Smithsonian

LITTLE EXPLORER

A **4D** BOOK

BUZZING BEES

by Melissa Higgins

PEBBLE
a capstone imprint

 Capstone 4D
Education

1. Ask an adult to download the app.

2. Scan any page with the star.

3. Enjoy your cool stuff!

OR

Use this password at capstone4D.com

bees.03413

Little Explorer is published by Pebble,
1710 Roe Crest Drive, North Mankato, Minnesota 56003
www.mycapstone.com

Library of Congress Cataloging-in-Publication Data
Names: Higgins, Melissa, 1953- author.
Title: Buzzing bees : a 4D book / by Melissa Higgins.
Description: North Mankato, Minnesota : Pebble, [2019] | Series:
    Little entomologist 4D | Audience: Age 4-8. | Audience: K to
    Grade 3. | Includes bibliographical references and index.
Identifiers: LCCN 2018041893| ISBN 9781977103413 (library
    binding) | ISBN 9781977105684 (paperback) | ISBN
    9781977103475 (ebook pdf)
Subjects: LCSH: Bees—Juvenile literature.
Classification: LCC QL565.2 .H54 2019 | DDC 638/.1—dc23
LC record available at https://lccn.loc.gov/2018041893

Editorial Credits

Abby Colich, editor; Kyle Grenz, designer; Kelly Garvin,
media researcher; Tori Abraham, production specialist

Our very special thanks to Gary Hevel, Public Information Officer
(Emeritus), Entomology Department, at the Smithsonian National
Museum of Natural History. Capstone would also like to thank
Kealy Gordon, Product Development Manager, and the following
at Smithsonian Enterprises: Ellen Nanney, Licensing Manager;
Brigid Ferraro, Vice President, Education and Consumer Products;
and Carol LeBlanc, Senior Vice President, Education and
Consumer Products.

Image Credits

Alamy: Genevieve Vallee, 27, Nature Collection, 23; Science Source/
Scott Camazine, 17; Shutterstock: Anna Morgan, 1, Bachkova Natalia,
7, Daniel Prudeck, 2, 13, dwphotos, 7 (top inset), Ed Phillips, 21,
Elliotte Rusty Harold, 29, Frank Reiser, 11 (top inset), Ian Grainger,
19, irin-k, 5, 25 (bottom inset), Jennifer Bosvert, 20, JSseng, 14, Marek
Mierzejewski, 5, Moolkum, 22, NoPainNoGain, 8, PYP, 11, Rosafandi
Rosli, 25, Sweet Crisis, 9, TB studio, cover

Printed and bound in the United States of America.
PA48

Table of Contents

The Buzz About Bees

Do you ever see bees buzzing around a flower? Bees are very important. They move pollen from one flower to another. This helps new plants grow. Without bees, Earth would have fewer plants.

About 25,000 species of bees live in almost all parts of the world. Some bees are social. They live with other bees in a hive. Other bees are solitary. They live and work alone.

— DID YOU KNOW? —

A bee's buzzing sound comes from the fast beating of its wings.

Parts of a Bee

Bees are insects. Bees have two pairs of wings. They also have two antennae and six legs. Some bees have hairy legs and stomachs. The hair collects pollen. Bees have long tongues for getting nectar from flowers.

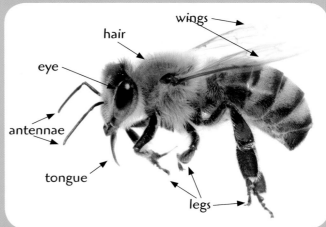

hair

wings

eye

antennae

tongue

legs

Bumble Bees

Number of species: 255
Found: Worldwide in mild climates
Length: 0.6 to 1 inch (1.5 to 2.5 centimeters)

Bumble bees are good pollinators. Their heavy bodies and fast-beating wings shake pollen from flowers. A worker collects pollen on her fuzzy stomach. She carries it back to the hive. Young bees eat the pollen. Bumble bee hives are often on or under the ground. About 50 to 200 bumble bees share a hive.

DID YOU KNOW?

Most bees flap their wings up and down. Bumble bees move their wings back and forth.

Inside a Hive

Three kinds of bees live in each hive. There are drones, workers, and a queen. Workers are all female. They gather pollen and feed young bees. They also protect the hive. Drones are male. They mate with the queen. The queen lays eggs.

Carpenter Bees

Number of species: More than 500
Found: Worldwide except in the coldest climates
Length: 0.5 to 1 inch (1.3 to 2.5 cm)

Carpenter bees make nests in wood. A female drills small holes. She lays an egg in each hole. Then she places a ball of pollen near the egg. The egg hatches into a larva. The larva eats the pollen.

Life Cycle of a Bee

A bee begins life as an egg. The egg hatches into a larva. The larva eats and eats until it becomes a pupa. An adult emerges from the pupa.

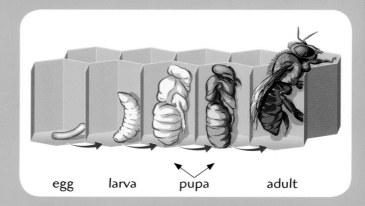

egg   larva   pupa   adult

Carpenter bees cut and tear into wood using mandibles. These are near the mouthparts on either side of the head.

DID YOU KNOW?

Carpenter bees can harm wooden buildings.

Cuckoo Bees

Number: 5 to 15 percent of all bees
Found: Worldwide except in the coldest climates
Length: 0.25 to 0.5 inch (0.6 to 1.3 cm)

Cuckoos steal nests from other bees. Some cuckoos lay an egg in another bee's nest. The cuckoo's egg hatches first. It eats food meant for the other bee's larvae. Sometimes the cuckoo even eats the other larvae.

Other cuckoos invade another queen's hive. They kill the strongest workers. Then they show other workers their stingers. The frightened workers let the cuckoos stay. Some cuckoos kill the queen. Others live alongside her.

neon cuckoo bee

Bee Stingers

Bees use their stingers to protect themselves. Most bees only sting when they feel threatened. Stingers contain venom. The venom slows down any predators. Only female bees have stingers. Some species don't have them at all.

Honey Bees

Number of species: 7
Found: Worldwide except Antarctica
Length: 0.3 to 0.7 inch (0.8 to 1.8 cm)

Honey bees are very social. A hive can have as many as 60,000 bees. Most of them are female workers. The workers do many jobs. Scouts look for food. Collectors gather pollen, nectar, or water. House bees turn nectar into honey. They also feed the queen and take care of young bees. Guard bees protect the hive from predators.

The Waggle Dance

Scouts have an interesting way to tell collectors when they've found food. They do a dance in the shape of the number 8. Scientists call this the waggle dance. The longer a scout dances, the farther away the food is.

Honey and Beeswax

Only honey bees make honey that people eat. Worker bees chew nectar until it turns into honey. They store the honey inside a honeycomb. The honeycomb is made from wax. The wax started out as honey. Worker bees have glands that turn honey into wax.

Honey bees are important pollinators. They make honey too. Beekeepers build boxes that are perfect for hives. They place the boxes near crops that need to be pollinated. Then they collect the honey to eat or to sell. But honey bees are in danger. Diseases kill them. Mites and pesticides do too. Scientists are working to help protect honey bees.

Killer Bees

Number of species: 1
Found: South America, Central America, and southern
     United States
Length: 0.3 to 0.7 inch (0.8 to 1.8 cm)

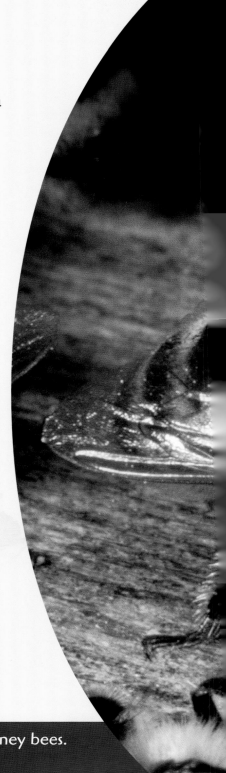

Killer bees are a strain of honey bees. Killer bees are very bold. They swarm faster than other bees. They travel in larger numbers too. When they feel threatened, they chase far and long. Killer bees have the same amount of venom as honey bees. Victims can get thousands of stings. That many stings can kill an adult human.

DID YOU KNOW?
Killer bees have killed hundreds of humans.

Killer bees are also called Africanized honey bees.

Escaped Bees

In 1957 a scientist in Brazil wanted to create bees that could make more honey. His bees escaped from the lab. They have moved north every year. Killer bees now live in the southern United States. The bees will keep moving until they reach places where it's too cold for them.

Leafcutter Bees

Number of species: 4,100
Found: Worldwide mostly in warm climates
Length: 0.4 to 0.8 inch (1 to 2 cm)

Leafcutter bees live alone. A female finds holes in logs, stems, or the ground. She lines each hole with leaves. She lays an egg in each hole. Then she plugs the hole with more leaves. This helps keep out predators. Her larvae eat pollen that she has left in the hole. Most young leafcutter bees stay in their nests over the winter. They grow into adults. They bite through the leaf plugs and come out in the spring.

DID YOU KNOW?

Mason bees are related to leafcutter bees. They use mud to make their nests instead of leaves.

Leafcutter bees cut round holes in leaves.

Bees on the Menu

Many animals eat bees. At least 24 kinds of birds eat them. Bears, weasels, and mice do too. Lizards, frogs, and toads might make a meal of adult bees or their young. Some insects and spiders eat bees as well.

Mining Bees

Number of species: 1,500
Found: Worldwide mostly in warm climates
Length: 0.3 to 0.7 inch (0.8 to 1.8 cm)

Mining bees dig holes in soil. A female makes a special liquid. Then she lines the hole with it. After the liquid dries, she rubs the dirt walls with her stomach. This polishes the soil. It becomes a sturdy and smooth nest for her young.

DID YOU KNOW?

Some mining bees like company. Tens of thousands might build their nests close together.

Mining bees often dig their nests near shrubs.
Each entrance is marked with a small mound of soil.

Oil-Collecting Bees

Number of species: 26
Found: South Africa
Length: 0.2 to 0.5 inch (0.5 cm to 1.3 cm)

Oil-collecting bees only visit snapdragon flowers. These bees have very long legs. Their feet are covered with soft hairs. The hairs soak up oil from the flower. Females use the oil to line their nests. They also mix the oil with pollen. It makes a kind of bread. The bees feed it to their young.

snapdragon flowers

DID YOU KNOW?

Oil-collecting bees build their nests underground.

Vulture Bees

Number of species: 3
Found: North and South America
Length: Up to 0.2 inch (0.5 cm)

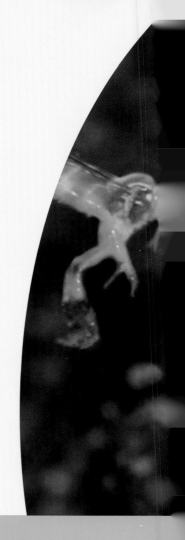

Vulture bees do not feed on pollen or nectar. They eat the meat of dead animals. They also eat the eggs and larvae of wasps and toads. Vulture bees have sharp mouths. They work like teeth. Females mix meat with their saliva. It forms a goo. The goo is healthy for their young.

Bee or Wasp?

Bees and wasps belong to the same group. Like most bees, female wasps have stingers with venom. But unlike most bees, wasps eat meat. Wasps have no hairs or pockets for collecting pollen. Their smooth, thin bodies are perfect for chasing prey.

bee

wasp

Stingless Bees

Number of species: 500
Found: Worldwide mostly in tropical climates
Length: 0.2 inch (0.5 cm)

Stingless bees do have stingers. But the stingers are very small. They can't hurt anyone they sting. They protect their hives in other ways. Some stingless bees use soldiers. These female workers guard a hive's entrance. They use strong mandibles to bite invaders. A soldier will not let go of an enemy. The bee may even hang on until it dies.

stingless bees in their nest

Sweat Bees

Number of species: 4,300
Found: Every continent except Antarctica
Length: 0.1 to 0.5 inch (0.3 to 1.3 cm)

Sweat bees are attracted to human sweat. Many people consider these bees pests and swat them away. Luckily, sweat bees don't often sting.

Some sweat bees are social. They live in a hive with a queen. But most are solitary. Each female builds her own nests. The nests are often underground. Some sweat bees are both social and solitary. Several females share a hive.

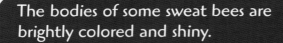

The bodies of some sweat bees are brightly colored and shiny.

Becoming a Queen

Queen bees let off a scent when they get old. This tells worker bees it's time for a new queen. Worker bees start feeding a special food to female larvae. These bees grow into queens. New queens fight to the death until only one remains.

Glossary

gland (GLAND)—an organ in the body that makes certain chemicals

larva (LAR-vuh)—an insect at the stage of development between an egg and an adult

mandible (MAN-duh-buhl)—strong mouthparts used to chew

mate (MATE)—to join together to produce young

mite (MITE)—tiny animals in the subclass *Arachnida*

nectar (NEK-tur)—a sweet liquid that some insects collect from flowers and eat as food

pesticide (PES-tuh-side)—a poisonous chemical used to kill insects, rats, and fungi that can damage plants

pollen (POL-uhn)—a powder flowers make to help them create new seeds

predator (PRED-uh-tur)—an animal that hunts other animals for food

prey (PRAY)—an animal hunted by another animal for food

social (SOH-shuhl)—living in groups or packs

solitary (SOL-uh-ter-ee)—living and hunting alone

species (SPEE-seez)—a group of living things that can reproduce with one another

swarm (SWARM)—to gather or fly close together in a large group

venom (VEN-uhm)—a poisonous liquid produced by some animals

Critical Thinking Questions

1. How many known species of bees are in the world? Where do they live?

2. Killer bees look like honey bees. In what ways are they different? Use the text to help you with your answer.

3. In what ways are bees helpful?

Read More

Esbaum, Jill. *Honey Bees.* Explore My World. Washington, D.C.: National Geographic Kids, 2017.

Marsh, Laura. *Bees.* Washington, D.C.: National Geographic, 2016.

Unstead, Sue. *Amazing Bees.* New York: DK Publishing, 2016.

Internet Sites

Use FactHound to find Internet sites related to this book.

Visit *www.facthound.com*

Just type in 9781977103413 and go.

 Check out projects, games and lots more at
www.capstonekids.com

Index